The Story of RABBI YISROEL SALANTER

MOSAICA PRESS

RABBI DR. ZALMAN F. URY

Mosaica Press, Inc.
© 2017 by Jewish Content Inc.
Designed by Rayzel Broyde
Typeset by Brocha Mirel Strizower
Illustrations by Dena Ackerman

All rights reserved
ISBN-10: 1-946351-08-3
ISBN-13: 978-1-946351-08-1

No part of this book may be used or reproduced or transmitted in any form or by any means, electronic or mechanical, including photocopying, recording, or by any information storage and retrieval system, without written permission from the publisher.

Published and distributed by:
Mosaica Press, Inc.
www.mosaicapress.com
info@mosaicapress.com

TABLE OF CONTENTS

Preface 5
Foreword to the First Edition 8
About the Author 10
Chapter One: The Development of a Great Leader 17
Chapter Two: Doing Great Things 32
Chapter Three: Little Things Count Too 69
Chapter Four: Some of Reb Yisroel's Favorite Sayings 83
Chapter Five: Food for Thought 86
Chapter Six: Some Suggestions for Becoming a Better Person . . . 92

PREFACE

THE STORY OF RABBI YISROEL SALANTER was first published in 1971 by our dear father, Rabbi Dr. Zalman F. Ury, *zt"l*, in conjunction with Torah Umesorah Publications. The book was reprinted twice — in 1976 and again in 1981. The book is now out of print and unavailable. We thank Torah Umesorah for granting us the right to reprint this work.

Our goal with the reprinting of this book is to once again make it available to the young reader. This book is an excellent way to introduce young people to the concepts of *mussar* (Jewish ethics) and hopefully to help them assimilate these principles into their daily lives.

Rather than merely reprinting the original book, we decided to update the book to make it more appealing to today's generation of youngsters. The original text and illustrations are now forty-five years old, and much has changed in the style of writing of children's books and in the style of illustrations that young people find appealing. We attempted to stick to the original text as much as possible, but we made changes where the use of language has changed or where a new idiom seemed appropriate.

The illustrations in this version of *The Story of Rabbi Yisroel Salanter* are all new, executed in the medium of pencil and paper by the very talented Mrs. Dena Ackerman. Reb Yisroel's kindness and compassion come through in these illustrations, giving them a loving, warm glow. An effort was made to make them as authentic as possible, conforming to the look and feel of nineteenth-century Jewish Eastern Europe. The most challenging aspect was coming up with a look for Reb Yisroel himself. There are no extant paintings or photographs of Reb Yisroel — only descriptions of his meticulous mode of dress. Some have said that his son, Rabbi Yitzchok Lipkin, resembled him. Photographs of Rabbi Yitzchok Lipkin exist, so we used these as a starting point to portray Reb Yisroel's visage. We thank Mrs. Ackerman for her exquisite artistry and for her pleasant demeanor, even in the face of our many comments and requests.

Following this preface, you will find the original foreword by Dr. Joseph Kaminetsky, the first director of Torah Umesorah and a pioneer in establishing Jewish day schools in America. Immediately after is a new section, titled "About the Author," which gives a brief life history of our father, *zt"l*, and explains his connection and devotion to *mussar* and to Reb Yisroel Salanter. It is written for youngsters and is the point in the book where children should begin reading. Mrs. Ackerman has done an excellent illustration of our father for this section that projects his warm character.

Thanks go to our publisher, Rabbi Yaacov Haber of Mosaica Press, for agreeing to undertake this project and for his guiding hand in determining the correct voice for this updated version of the original work. Thanks also go to Rabbi Doron Kornbluth of Mosaica Press for his skillful editing of the manuscript and for his expert advice. The beautiful, all-new graphics and professional layout are due to the artistic talent and dedication of Mrs. Rayzel Broyde, whom we thank for her fine work. We also thank Mrs. Beena (Ury) Sklare for the lovely cover by which this book may rightfully be judged. Our gratitude goes to Mrs. Sherie Gross and to her team of proofreaders and copyeditors who toiled hard to bring this book to a more perfect state. Finally, we thank the Ribbono Shel Olam for helping us preserve the legacy of Rabbi Yisroel Salanter and our dear father, *zt"l*.

Rabbi Hoshea and Celia (Ury) Rabinowitz
Rabbi Moshe and Natalie (Ury) Amster
Dr. Robert and Ramma (Ury) Hoffnung
Dr. Yisrael and Gittie Ury

FOREWORD TO THE FIRST EDITION

Dr. Joseph Kaminetsky, National Director, Torah Umesorah

WE ARE HAPPY TO PRESENT ANOTHER volume in our series of *Gedolim* for young people, *The Story of Rabbi Yisroel Salanter* by Rabbi Dr. Zalman F. Ury.

Dr. Ury, who is a chief consultant at the Bureau of Jewish Education of Greater Los Angeles, spent many years as principal of various Hebrew day schools across the country. He knows our day schools very well and even now concentrates his endeavors on the day schools in the Los Angeles area, guiding them in their curricular problems and in all other facets of their work.

He is also the author of learned studies on the philosophy of the Mussar Movement as we know it today and of which Reb Yisroel was the originator. Dr. Ury has skillfully distilled all of his findings, studies, and articles on this great sage into this concise, simple volume that is calculated to give our pupils a good idea of who Reb Yisroel was, how he lived by his ideals, and how he implemented the principles of *mussar* in his daily life.

In reading this volume, our pupils will also get a good picture of life as it was lived in the European *shtetl*, of what problems the Jews faced under the Russian Czar, and how the yeshiva student sought to perfect himself through the study of *mussar*. The volume depicts many of the important as well as the lesser known incidents in the life of Reb Yisroel and gives a clear-cut presentation of his philosophy and the principles by which he lived. Especially urgent are the final two chapters, prodding the reader to apply these principles to his own life.

In an age when the most important heritage we can give our pupils is an understanding of the ethical ideas and values of Judaism, this volume is a most vital contribution. We do hope that it will be read, studied, and reread by all yeshiva students.

ABOUT THE AUTHOR

RABBI DR. ZALMAN F. URY WAS born in 1924 in a small town in Poland called Stoiptz. His original family name was Fajwosowich (pronounced "five-oh-sovich"), but many years later, when already in the United States, he changed his last name to Ury because no one could pronounce Fajwosowich! He kept the letter "F" as his middle initial as a reminder of his original family name.

As a young boy, he loved to read and also enjoyed playing soccer with his friends. He learned to read Hebrew at an early age and read a Hebrew book of *midrashim* on the *parshah* from cover to cover. As his learning advanced, he began to spend time with much older boys and joined the local chapter of the Tiferes Bachurim learning group. Meanwhile, his uncle, Yeshaya "Shaya" Borishansky, *hy"d*, was learning in the famous yeshiva in Kletsk, headed by Rabbi Aharon Kotler, *zt"l*. Shaya was one of the yeshiva's top *bachurim* and Rabbi Kotler's *chavrusa*. Every time Shaya visited his sister (Zalman's mother) in Stoiptz, he noticed how his young nephew was developing into a young *talmid chacham*. One day, when Zalman was only ten years old, Shaya told his sister that he wanted to take young Zalman with him to learn in the yeshiva. After his parents discussed it, Zalman was allowed to travel with his uncle to far-away Kletsk to begin learning in the yeshiva.

When Zalman first got to Kletsk, he missed his parents and began to cry, but it didn't take too long until he felt very much at home inside the four walls of the *beis medrash*. He would visit home for Yom Tov (and of course went home for his bar mitzvah) but otherwise spent all his time in the yeshiva. He became very close to the Rosh Yeshiva and would attend his *shiurim*, which were several hours long and very complicated.

The yeshiva did not have a dormitory or a dining room, so it arranged places for the *bachurim* to stay and families with whom the *bachurim* could eat. Usually, a *bachur* would eat regularly on Sundays with one family, Mondays with another family, etc. This arrangement was known as *essen teg*, literally "eating days." Sometimes, on Shabbos, he would eat at the home of Rabbi Elazar Shach, *zt"l*, who later would become the most influential rabbi of his time.

During one of his years in the yeshiva, Zalman was fortunate to live in the home of the yeshiva's *Mashgiach Ruchani*, Rabbi Yosef Aryeh Leib Nanedik, *hy"d*. The Mashgiach was a *talmid* of the Alter of Kelm, who in turn was one of the main *talmidim* of Rabbi Yisroel Salanter. The Mashgiach was a master of *mussar*, and by living in his house, young Zalman had the opportunity to learn more about Rabbi Yisroel Salanter and to observe firsthand how a *baal mussar* leads his life. Thus began Rabbi Ury's devotion to Rabbi Salanter's teachings and his quest to share them with other Jews.

The Second World War began on September 1, 1939, and with it began the terrible destruction of Jewish Europe. Poland was divided between Nazi Germany and the Soviet Union. Fortunately, Kletsk and Stoiptz were on the Soviet side, so the Jews there did not face an immediate danger of being killed. Many of the yeshivos realized that it was no longer safe to stay in Poland, so they moved to Vilna, the capital of Lithuania, which was neutral at the time. The Kletsk yeshiva also decided to relocate to Vilna, so they asked all the *bachurim* to first go home and ask permission of their parents to move to Lithuania. At fifteen years old, Zalman went home for Shabbos and got his parents' blessing to make the trip to Vilna. It was the last time he saw his family, as they were all killed in the war.

In Vilna, Zalman was able to continue his learning, but his freedom did not last long. In June 1940, the Soviets invaded Lithuania and imposed communist rule. Under communism, it was illegal to teach Torah and the *bachurim* had to learn secretly. Many of the *bachurim* applied to get visas to leave the

Soviet Union. Even though doing so was legal, the government accused them of treason for trying to leave!

One Friday night in June 1941, at three in the morning, Zalman heard a knock on his door. It was the Soviet police arresting him! He was told that he was being sent to Siberia for his "crime." The hard-labor camp in Siberia where he was sent was a terrible place where many of the inmates died. But Zalman realized that being sent to Siberia was a miracle from Hashem, for as the train taking him to Siberia pulled out of Vilna, the Nazis had just begun invading. Had he remained in Vilna, he certainly would have perished.

After being released from prison, Zalman and some of his fellow yeshiva *bachurim* travelled to Uzbekistan, which was part of the Soviet Union but a relatively safe place for Jews. He secretly taught Torah to young Jewish boys who also had somehow made it to Uzbekistan. One of those boys is now a Rosh Yeshiva in Israel!

Soon after the war ended in 1945, Zalman married a girl named Chava Perl who was also a refugee from Poland. By early 1947, with the help of Rabbi Kotler, *zt"l*, the young couple with their newborn baby daughter finally arrived in Lakewood, New Jersey. Rabbi Kotler had relocated the yeshiva from Kletsk to Lakewood and named it Beth Medrash Govoha. Rabbi Ury learned in the *kollel* in Beth Medrash Govoha, where he received his *semichah* from the Rosh Yeshiva.

Rabbi Ury felt a strong responsibility to teach Torah to Jewish children and got his first teaching job in St. Louis, Missouri. When he arrived in St. Louis, he did not even speak English, so he took classes in English so that he could better communicate with his students and their parents. He also took classes in education, earned a college degree, and eventually became the principal of the school where he taught.

The Ury family moved to Los Angeles in 1957 where Rabbi Ury became principal of another Jewish school. A few years later he took a position with the Bureau of Jewish Education, which was responsible for education in all the Orthodox schools in Los Angeles. Within a few years he became rabbi of the Young Israel of Beverly Hills, where he became famous for his *shiurim* and his *drashos*. At the same time, he earned a master's degree and a Doctorate in Education. What was the subject of his doctoral dissertation? The *mussar* of Rabbi Yisroel Salanter, of course!

Throughout the years, Rabbi Ury corresponded with many great rabbis and wrote dozens of articles on *chidushei Torah* and on Jewish education. He published his collected work on *chidushei Torah* and *mussar* in a *sefer* called *Kedushas Avraham*, named for his father, *hy"d*. He also published the first version of this book, *The Story of Rabbi Yisroel Salanter*, so that children could learn about *mussar* and the incredible work of Rabbi Yisroel Salanter.

After working more than four decades for the Bureau of Jewish Education, Rabbi Ury decided to retire and fulfill his lifelong dream of living in Israel. In 1993 on a visit to Israel, Rabbi Ury went to Rabbi Shach and told him that he had retired from his job and about his plans to move to Israel. Rabbi Shach responded to him: "You can't abandon *chinuch*. Go back to your job in Los Angeles." Rabbi Ury listened to Rabbi Shach and went back to the Bureau of Jewish Education, where he worked for thirteen more years until his death.

Rabbi Ury — Zalman ben Avraham Halevi — returned his

neshamah to Hashem in 5766 (2006) on the twenty-fifth day of Shevat — the very day of Rabbi Yisroel Salanter's *yahrzeit*! He is buried in Yerushalayim in Har Hamenuchos. May his legacy be a lesson for all of us.

- *Chapter One* -

THE DEVELOPMENT OF A GREAT LEADER

YOUNG GENIUS TO SPIRITUAL GIANT

Rabbi Zev Wolf Lipkin, a descendant of the Gaon of Vilna and a well-known Talmudic scholar, served as rabbi in several Lithuanian communities. He was the author of a commentary on *Shas* known as *Hagahos Ben Aryeh* and other important *sefarim*. His wife, Leah, was a most unusual *rebbetzin*. She was gentle, considerate, and scholarly. Rebbetzin Lipkin had mastered the *Tanach* and was knowledgeable in many areas of Jewish learning. The people of her town, as well as those in other communities, respected and loved her for her kindness and charitable work.

On the sixth day of Cheshvan 5571 (November 3, 1810), a boy was born into this family in the town of Zhagory. The boy was named Yisroel.

In those days, it was customary for learned fathers to teach their own sons Torah. Yisroel was lucky to have two teachers, not just one:

- His father taught him Torah and the observance of *mitzvos*.
- His mother trained him to be kind, to respect the rights and feelings of others, and to always have a sense of responsibility to Hashem.

How delighted and happy the parents must have been with their young son, who was an eager student and remembered everything he was taught. Rabbi Zev Wolf proudly predicted that Yisroel would one day be a great *talmid chacham*. It did not take long for Yisroel to make his father's prediction come true. At the age of ten, Yisroel began delivering learned *shiurim*, known as *pilpul*, to audiences of adults. By now, everybody agreed that young Yisroel was a genius!

When Yisroel reached the age of twelve, his father realized that the time had come to send his bright son to study with a great rabbi.

After careful consideration, Rabbi Zev Wolf sent his son to the famous Rabbi Zvi Hirsch Braude of Salant.

The town of Salant had many well-known scholars. Young Yisroel soon found many admirers among them. But no one admired him more than his master, the great Rabbi Braude. The rabbi of Salant spent more time teaching the young lad than any of his other students. When Yisroel became bar mitzvah, Rabbi Braude allowed him to deliver *shiurim* at the local yeshiva.

Once, when Yisroel was about fourteen years old, he composed an original essay of *chidushei Torah*. At the suggestion of his rebbe, Yisroel sent a copy of it to the sage, Rabbi Akiva Eiger of Posen. It is reported that this famous rabbi praised

the *chidushei Torah* of young Yisroel as a scholarly masterpiece befitting a real genius.

In those times, it was customary to get married young. Yisroel became engaged at the age of fourteen. The father of the bride, in keeping with the practice of the time, promised a dowry of 300 rubles. Unfortunately, the bride's father, having suffered a serious financial loss, was unable to make good on his pledge.

The father of the bride, Reb Yaakov Eisenstein of Salant, now a poor man, felt that he had no right to insist upon the marriage. A dowry was very important to a young scholar like Yisroel, for it would enable him to study Torah day and night without having to worry about making a living. And so, Reb Yaakov, though he very much wanted Yisroel as his son-in-law, began having second thoughts about the forthcoming marriage.

While Reb Yaakov Eisenstein and his family were gloomily considering the possible broken engagement, a new development came about that tempted them to give up their claim on the young genius. A rich man, who had heard about the unfortunate financial condition of the Eisensteins, offered them the fabulous sum of 10,000 rubles if they would release Yisroel from his obligation to marry their daughter. This wealthy man planned to offer Yisroel his daughter as a wife, together, of course, with a big dowry.

The Eisenstein family now faced a very difficult situation. The parents, and especially their daughter, still wanted to go through with the marriage. But they were tormented by thoughts of perpetual poverty. How would the young scholar study Torah if he had no income? How long could the

Eisenstein family go on suffering from poverty? Here was an opportunity to get away from poverty and become respectable again. Shouldn't they accept the 10,000 rubles for the good of everyone involved?

No final decision was reached. Reb Yaakov Eisenstein traveled to Zhagory, Yisroel's home town. There he met with the Lipkin family to discuss the planned marriage of their children. Reb Yaakov told the Lipkins that he was ready, though reluctant, to give up his daughter's claim to marry Yisroel.

But the Lipkins, and especially Yisroel, would have none of this. An engagement, they said, is a solemn pledge, not to be broken for the sake of money.

In other words, the Lipkin family was ready to choose a life of poverty rather than a life of comfort and wealth attained through a broken promise. "Let us set the date of our children's wedding," said Rabbi Lipkin. Wine was served amidst joyous expressions of *mazal tov* and *l'chayim*.

After their wedding, Reb Yisroel and his young wife settled in Salant, where they lived for a number of years. She operated a small store and supported their growing family while her husband spent all of his time studying Torah. The family remained poor but happy, knowing that they had chosen Torah with honor instead of Torah and money without honor.

Reb Yisroel soon became famous throughout the Jewish world as a *gaon*. Many wealthy people wanted to offer him lavish gifts, but he refused to accept them. Leading Jewish communities (*kehilos*) invited him to serve as their Chief Rabbi, but he preferred to study Torah in the quiet surroundings of his Salant home.

Though his last name was Lipkin, he became known as Reb Yisroel Salanter, which means Rabbi Yisroel from Salant. Why?

Because it was in Salant that the young genius blossomed into a spiritual giant and became one of the great rabbis and leaders of the Jewish people.

MEETING IN THE FOREST

Salant, a typical Lithuanian *shtetl,* prided itself on its many learned men. There was one *talmid chacham,* however, who went unnoticed for years. Were it not for Reb Yisroel, who discovered this man's greatness and saintliness, it is likely that no one would have ever known that a legendary *tzaddik* walked the streets of Salant. The name of this mysterious and hidden *tzaddik* was Rabbi Yoseph Zundel, better known as Reb Zundel.

When Yoseph Zundel was still a child, he showed great intelligence, a keen sense of morality, and a strong inclination to matters of holiness. Rabbi Yoseph Zundel studied in the famous Yeshiva of Volozhin. There he became one of the most trusted students of Rabbi Chaim Volozhiner, the famous student of the Gaon of Vilna and the founder of the Yeshiva in Volozhin.

Reb Zundel was a very humble man. Though great in Torah, he did not consider himself worthy of the position of a rabbi. So he chose to be a small merchant, and at times he did manual work, struggling to make a living. He dressed like an average person, unlike other rabbis, because he wanted to remain humble and unnoticed.

Reb Zundel obeyed all *mitzvos* with great care. For example, he was so strict in observing the Fifth Commandment (*kibud av v'em* — "you shall honor your father and your mother") that he himself once paved a muddy alley so that his mother would not soil her shoes on her way to shul. Yet to the people of Salant, Reb Zundel was an ordinary person — a little special, but not great.

When young Yisroel Lipkin came to Salant, he became attracted to Reb Zundel. Somehow, the young genius sensed that Reb Zundel was no average person. He began observing and watching Reb Zundel and noticed that he would often be silent, and at times would disappear. This interested the young scholar and he decided to follow Reb Zundel. Yisroel thought that there was something special and mysterious about this man. Is he one of the *lamed-vovniks*, the mysterious thirty-six saintly men, wondered Yisroel? After the young boy "discovered" Reb Zundel's greatness, many people too began regarding him as a legendary *tzaddik* or a *lamed-vovnik*.

Reb Zundel would frequently leave town and walk about the surrounding fields and forests. There he would study *mussar*, *daven*, and think about his duties to Hashem and man. The young Yisroel began following Reb Zundel. Standing at a distance, unobserved, he would watch Reb Zundel intensely. The *tzaddik davened*, swaying back and forth. Sometimes he wept; on other occasions he was full of joy. Yisroel would sometimes hear Reb Zundel say things to himself. Yisroel could only overhear a few isolated words like "restraint," "self-control," "fight," and similar expressions.

One day, they met in the forest. Reb Zundel, turning suddenly to the young Yisroel, exclaimed: "Yisroel, study *mussar* so that you may become a *yerei shamayim*!" This moment, recalled Rabbi Yisroel Salanter years later, became the turning point in his life. From then on Reb Zundel became Reb Yisroel's model and master in *mussar*. Both the older scholar and the younger

one could no longer remain in their comfortable and private little worlds. The young Reb Yisroel, by openly becoming Reb Zundel's student, made his master's saintliness known. Still, it was the young student who became even more famous as a master in *mussar* thanks to the strong influence of the legendary Reb Zundel.

BECOMING ROSH YESHIVA

Reb Yisroel had refused many offers to serve as rabbi, but when he was invited to become the Rosh Yeshiva of the well-known Rabbi Mailo's yeshiva in Vilna, he accepted the appointment gladly. Reb Yisroel, like his father, was an educator at heart. So when he was given an opportunity to teach — especially in Vilna, known as the "Jerusalem of Lithuania" (*Yerushalayim d'Lita*) — he must have been very happy indeed.

Reb Yisroel Salanter moved to Vilna, the city where the Vilna Gaon had lived, hoping to teach Talmud and *mussar* there as he had learned them from Reb Zundel. Vilna, the city of *talmidei chachachim*, was very pleased with Reb Yisroel, for he proved himself a master teacher. His fame spread. He began lecturing in the local shuls, teaching the people the importance of *mussar* and proper conduct, and his audiences grew larger and larger.

One day, Reb Yisroel surprised everyone by announcing that he was resigning from his honored post as Rosh Yeshiva. It seemed that Reb Yisroel was more popular with the students of the yeshiva than Rabbi Mordechai Meltzer, also a Rosh Yeshiva in the same school, was. Reb Yisroel, realizing that he was indirectly hurting the feelings of Rabbi Meltzer, felt compelled to give up his important and well-paying position.

Again he chose Torah with honor and refused to hurt other people, even though it meant giving up his livelihood. He practiced what he preached.

THE BEIS HAMUSSAR

After leaving the yeshiva, Reb Yisroel remained in Vilna for some time. He moved to the suburb of Zarece, where he opened a yeshiva of his own. This yeshiva was different from the other yeshivos because he introduced there the study of *mussar*. This school became the first *mussar* yeshiva in Lithuania. Later, more yeshivos followed its example. Today, *mussar* is studied in most yeshivos.

Reb Yisroel set up a special room in the yeshiva for the study of *mussar*, known as the Beis Hamussar. This was a simple room containing various *mussar sefarim*, where students would study *mussar*, either individually or in groups.

Reb Yisroel did not limit his teaching activities to the yeshiva students. He continued delivering his *mussar* lectures in shuls throughout Lithuania. He was a great speaker. He would inspire his audiences to serve Hashem not only through prayer and the study of Torah, but also by dealing honestly and kindly with each other.

The shuls would be filled with eager audiences who would arrive even before the announced time. Sometimes, when the shul was packed with people, it was impossible for Reb Yisroel to enter. The people, who loved their saintly rabbi, would form a line of human hands carrying him overhead from hand to hand until he reached the front of the shul. It is reported that many individuals became *baalei teshuvah* as a result of Reb Yisroel's lectures.

Reb Yisroel organized groups of *baalei batim*, ordinary Jews, who would study *mussar*. He also set up special *mussar* study rooms. Such a room, as we have already mentioned, was known as a Beis Hamussar.

THE TRAVELING RABBI

After some time, Reb Yisroel had to leave Vilna because he ran into trouble with the Czarist authorities. The full story of his struggle with the cruel Russian government will be described in the following chapter. He had another important reason for leaving the city of Vilna. He had reached a decision: he would become a traveling rabbi. Why?

Reb Yisroel, who continuously examined his own conduct, became convinced that his mission could not be limited to Vilna alone. *There are so many Jewish communities who need mussar guidance*, he thought. He said: "The world exists for the sake of *chessed*. Anyone who has the power to influence others to become kinder and more religious is not allowed to sit back and only take care of his own spiritual needs."

As soon as Reb Yisroel would reach a decision, he would not rest until he carried it out. To become a traveling rabbi was no ordinary decision, and it wouldn't take a short time to implement. For as long as there were Jews in need of his *mussar* teachings, his task would not be completed. And so Reb Yisroel began a lifelong series of travels.

No other nineteenth century rabbi traveled as much as Rabbi Yisroel Salanter. His travels would separate him from his family for long periods of time, and because of this he and his family would suffer additional burdens of poverty. Quite often, he was in poor health. Yet, Reb Yisroel did not give up his mission. Neither poverty nor illness would stop him from bringing the word of Hashem to those who were spiritually poor. Reb Yisroel was always ready to sacrifice all he had for the sake of others.

Just as B'nei Yisrael wandered in the desert for forty long years, so did Reb Yisroel travel throughout Europe's Jewish communities. His many years of traveling, however, were not a punishment but a blessing for all those who came under his influence.

His first stop was Kovno, Lithuania's second capital. Before Reb Yisroel came there, Kovno was a stronghold of nonreligious groups. After he spent several years in the city, a strong Orthodox Jewish community developed there.

Reb Yisroel improved the spirit of the poor and lectured to the masses in the shuls. His personality and outstanding *drashos* attracted and influenced many people.

Reb Yisroel introduced the study of *mussar* in the local yeshivos. Realizing that bright scholars who were poor could not continue their studies after marriage, he formed a new type of yeshiva, called a *kollel,* where the scholars were paid to continue their studies. This school for married young scholars, called *Kollel Haperushim*, was established in the suburb of Slobodka (where the great Slobodka Yeshiva existed until the Nazis destroyed it during World War II). Reb Yisroel's *kollel* was successful in training outstanding rabbis.

In Kovno, Reb Yisroel formed *mussar* study groups for scholars. There he met many known rabbis who became his followers. Among them were Rabbi Yitzchak Blazer and Rabbi Naftali Amsterdam.

His travels brought him to many communities. Wherever he went, he would examine the religious and moral life of the

Jewish community. In Paris, for example, where many Jews had strayed from Yiddishkeit, Reb Yisroel spent two years. Though he was about seventy years old and sick, he labored hard in the French capital. He installed one of his *talmidim*, Rabbi Yehoshua Heschel Levin, as rabbi of the community. He improved the *kashrus* situation by bringing a *shochet* to Paris and opening a Jewish dairy to provide *cholov Yisroel*. Reb Yisroel also built a *mikveh*, schools for the young, and organized adult study groups to learn Torah and *mussar*.

Reb Yisroel spent many years in Germany where Orthodox Judaism was struggling against nonreligious groups. He visited many German Jewish communities, including Berlin, Frankfurt am Main, Halberstadt, Memel, Koenigsberg, and many more. He worked closely with the leaders of the German Jewish community, such as Rabbi Samson Raphael Hirsch, Rabbi Azriel Hildesheimer, and Dr. Meyer Lehmann. They and other leaders found in Reb Yisroel a true friend who understood their problems and was always ready to assist them. In order to communicate better with German Jews, who did not understand Yiddish, Reb Yisroel learned to speak German.

When Reb Yisroel came to the German city of Memel, he found very little observance of *mitzvos* there. Slowly and gradually he influenced some people who worked on Shabbos and Yom Tov to become *shomrei Shabbos*. Finding no Orthodox shul in Memel, Reb Yisroel decided to build one. After several years of effort, Reb Yisroel's beautiful shul was completed. Many famous rabbis came to the *chanukas habayis*, the dedication ceremonies. One of the guest speakers was the great Rabbi Meir Leibush Kaempner, author of the famous commentary on the entire Tanach known as *Malbim*. The *Malbim* paid a well-deserved compliment to Reb

Yisroel by paraphrasing the first line of *Mah Tovu*, the daily opening prayer. He said: "How good are your tents, Yaakov, when in your dwelling places there lives a Yisroel."

The shul Reb Yisroel built in Memel had a special adjoining dormitory for poor yeshiva students. This was something new in those days and it showed how much Reb Yisroel was concerned about students.

Wherever he came, he would meet with yeshiva students and lecture to them on Talmud and *mussar*. But Reb Yisroel also lectured to university students, many of whom became religious as a result of Reb Yisroel's teachings. This too was new and unheard of, for no other Lithuanian or Russian rabbi came in direct contact with college students.

During his long years of wandering, Reb Yisroel would occasionally return to his family and to the Russian Jewish communities. There he would study with his numerous students, lecture to the masses, and work for the welfare of the community. He would also attend emergency meetings of the Russian rabbis in the capital city of St. Petersburg.

Rabbi Yisroel Salanter spent the last few months of his life in Koenigsberg, the German city he used to visit frequently. He passed away on the 25th of Shevat, 5643 (February 2, 1883). He left no worldly goods to his children except his *tallis* and *tefillin*. Many outstanding rabbis and leaders came to Koenigsberg to attend his funeral. The rabbis who eulogized Rabbi Yisroel said that he was the greatest and saintliest man of his generation. Reb Yisroel was buried in Koenigsberg.

May his memory be blessed.

We have learned a little about Reb Yisroel's life. Now let's hear some stories about him and some of his famous sayings.

- *Chapter Two* -

DOING GREAT THINGS

EATING ON YOM KIPPUR?!

Have you ever heard of a great *tzaddik* reciting *kiddush*, drinking wine, and eating cake on Yom Kippur?

Here is one of the strangest Jewish stories ever told:

In the year 5608 (1848), there was a serious cholera epidemic in Vilna. Hundreds of people had died and the doctors were unable to control this terrible plague.

Cholera is a dreadful disease and very contagious. When someone would be stricken with it, few people were willing to take care of him — they simply feared for their own lives.

Not everyone who fell ill died, however. Some individuals did recover — those who had received proper medical care. Reb Yisroel Salanter knew that there was a great need for volunteers to care for the sick, especially the poor, who were the most neglected. And so he selected seventy of his most trusted yeshiva students, charging them with the responsibility to take care of poor patients who were not receiving proper care. The students were impressed by his request to undertake the task of saving lives (*pikuach nefesh*) and agreed to do the job.

However, their parents objected out of fear that their sons might become victims themselves.

Reb Yisroel knew that attending to the sick was a matter of life or death. He was not ready to give up. So he did something highly unusual and very risky: he guaranteed that all his seventy volunteers would return home safely — and they did!

The volunteers set out to fulfill the mitzvah of *bikur cholim*, visiting the sick. They helped many unfortunate families and saved lives. Of course, Reb Yisroel accompanied this group on its daily mercy missions.

The holy day of Yom Kippur of the year 5609 was approaching. Reb Yisroel was worried that many people who would be weakened from fasting on Yom Kippur would develop a low resistance and be stricken with cholera. Having worked with the sick, and after being advised by doctors, he was convinced that fasting on Yom Kippur would endanger many lives. He concluded that under such conditions, the Jews of Vilna must be told to eat on Yom Kippur. Since he was not an official rabbi in Vilna, Reb Yisroel approached the local rabbis and urged them to issue such a regulation. Some of the rabbis, though, did not agree with Reb Yisroel's suggestion.

But once again, he did not give up. He was convinced that since the epidemic threatened lives, the requirement of fasting on Yom Kippur must be set aside. He ordered his *talmidim* to post announcements in all the shuls calling on the people to refrain from fasting, shorten the *tefillos*, leave the shuls for periods of rest, and to assist those in need. However, the good Jews of Vilna were afraid to violate the sacred day of Yom Kippur and decided to fast.

On Yom Kippur, after *Shacharis* was finished in the shul where Reb Yisroel prayed, the *shamash* made the following announcement: "By the knowledge of *Hakadosh Baruch Hu*, and by the authority of the holy Torah, we grant permission, because of the plague, to eat and drink today."

A strange silence and a feeling of terror befell the congregation. No one moved and no one stirred. The men in the shul, each wrapped in his *tallis*, the women in the ladies' gallery, even the children — all stood there as if they were frozen and glued to the shul floor.

Then the people heard the voice of Reb Yisroel Salanter. All eyes turned toward the *bimah*, in the center of the shul, where he stood together with two other rabbis. He wept aloud and pleaded with the congregants, trying to convince them that this Yom Kippur is different. It is not eating that is forbidden today but rather fasting, argued Reb Yisroel. Still, the people had great reverence for Yom Kippur and hesitated. They did not move or make a sound.

He knew that the best way to teach someone is to set an example, so he ordered the *shamash* to bring wine and cake. Reb Yisroel and the other two rabbis then recited *kiddush*, drank a little wine, and ate small pieces of cake. Only then did the Jews of Vilna obey. They went home and broke the fast.

Years later, whenever Reb Yisroel would recall that Yom Kippur, he would express his pleasure at having done such a great mitzvah — saving lives. The Jews of Vilna never forgot his Yom Kippur *kiddush*.

DEFYING THE GOVERNMENT

The government of the Russian Czar (king) was anti-Semitic. The Jews suffered from many official restrictions.

The Jews and their religion were disliked and suspected by the Russians.

Some Jews, called *maskilim*, thought that if Jews would be less religious, the government might be more friendly to them. The motto of those non-religious Jews was: "Be a mentsch outside and a Jew at home." This meant that the Jew must not, for example, wear a *yarmulke* in public or speak Yiddish. He should dress like his non-Jewish neighbors, speak their language, eat their food, and socialize with them. At home, the Jew may keep a few *mitzvos* and speak Yiddish or Hebrew.

The rabbis, of course, considered the *maskilim* as enemies of the people and spirit of Israel. Naturally Reb Yisroel Salanter too opposed them. His motto was: "Be a mentsch and a Jew outside and a mentsch and a Jew at home." By this, he meant to teach the people that there is really no separation between "mentsch" and "Jew." The truly religious Jew, who follows the teachings of *mussar*, is a kind and good man. Therefore, the Jew should be proud of his religion and practice it in private as well as in public. He does not have to be taught by others how to be "good." Others should learn from him!

The *maskilim* convinced the Russian authorities that as long as the "old-fashioned" rabbis controlled the Jewish communities, there was little hope to change the Jewish religious way of life. As a result, the government opened two new rabbinical colleges to train "modern" rabbis. One of these schools was located in Vilna. In these colleges, the students were taught little Talmud. They studied many other subjects such as languages, literature, and history. The "rabbis" who graduated from those colleges were very different from the pious and learned Russian rabbis.

The rabbis opposed these schools, fearing that their graduates would be *am ha'aratzim* (ignorant) as far as real Jewish scholarship is concerned. They were proven right in Russia, as well as in Germany, where similar rabbinical colleges existed.

Meanwhile, the *maskilim*, seeking to impress the masses, invited Reb Yisroel to become the head of the new rabbinical college in Vilna. They knew that only someone like him, who commanded everyone's respect, would give the rabbinical college prestige and stop the rabbis' opposition. The *maskilim* had hoped that Reb Yisroel, who was so successful in teaching nonreligious Jews, would accept their offer to head the college as a challenge to bring nonreligious students closer to Judaism. But he understood that they were really trying to attack Torah and refused to accept this well-paying position.

The *maskilim* put much pressure on him. Uvarov, the Russian Minister of Education, became personally involved and ordered Reb Yisroel to accept the position. Remember that in those days Jews had no right to disobey the government. Those who disobeyed were severely punished without due process of law.

Reb Yisroel had no intention to yield on such a serious issue. Instead, he ran away from Vilna to Kovno to avoid having to accept the position. Of course, he knew that even there he would not be out of danger. He was ready to suffer the consequences instead of selling himself to the government in violation of his religious principles.

OBEYING THE LAW OF THE LAND

Though the Russian government was not friendly to its Jewish citizens, Reb Yisroel insisted that the law of the

land must be respected and obeyed by Jews too. This was based on a rule in the Talmud that states that laws passed by governments are to be obeyed (*dina demalchusa dina*).

Reb Yisroel once visited the town of Krinki. During the Shabbos *davening*, the *chazzan* did not recite the *tefillah* for the Welfare of the Czar and his government. Reb Yisroel objected, pointing out that our Sages said: "Pray for the welfare of the government."[1]

One of the restrictions placed on Jews was that they could not travel or live in certain parts of Russia. Jews were confined to what was then called "The Pale of Settlement." Only those Jews who were artisans or craftsmen received permission to travel and settle wherever they wished. Reb Yisroel, whose goal was to visit Jews wherever they were, had no permit to travel beyond The Pale of Settlement. Some Jews, considering this restriction as unfair, would travel illegally. Reb Yisroel was advised to do the same, but he did not want to break the law. He therefore decided to learn a trade that would grant him the right to travel. So this *tzaddik*, who spent all of his time learning Torah and doing *mitzvos*, decided to invest several weeks of his precious time learning to become an ink maker. After receiving a license to produce and sell ink, he was granted a permit for unrestricted travel and residence.

When Reb Yisroel published a rabbinical periodical, *Hatevunah*, he stated in the first issue that Jews are obliged to respect the government and obey its laws. A certain rabbi questioned how well he followed his own rules. He asked why Reb Yisroel did not accept the position of dean of the

---

1   *Avos* 3:2.

(non-Orthodox) rabbinical college in Vilna. "After all," argued the rabbi, "are you not supposed to respect the government and carry out its orders?"

Reb Yisroel replied that there is an important difference between obeying the law that restricts travel for Jews and accepting the position of dean. "In the case of the rabbinical college," he said, "the government threatened the religious welfare of the Jewish community by forcing it to accept unqualified rabbis. The government has no right to meddle in the internal religious affairs of the Jews. I, therefore, had the right to disobey.

"However, the law restricting Jews in travel and residence, though unfair and harmful to the Jews of Russia, is not a religious matter. This law deals with an economic matter, and the government, though it is unfriendly and discriminates against us, has the legal right to pass such a law. We must therefore obey it, though we know it is a bad law. Of course, we ought to try to change this law through proper legal channels. But as long as this law is in effect, we have no choice and must obey it.

"How then do you compare my rejection of the order to become dean of the rabbinical college to my obeying the law of restricted travel?" he asked. "The Russian government," emphasized Reb Yisroel, "has no right to tell the Jews how to train their rabbis. This is strictly a religious matter in which the government has neither the knowledge nor the right to interfere with us. I am sure you will agree with me that if the government would order us to desecrate Shabbos, we would have to disobey," he said. "If I had accepted the position of dean, I would have violated my religious convictions. No government has a right to demand from anyone to violate his religious principles," concluded Reb Yisroel.

SPIRITUAL BOOKKEEPING

A businessman or a company must have a system of bookkeeping for recording income, expenses, and profits. At the end of the year, a summary (known as an audit) of the activities of the year is made. The audit reveals important facts; for example, which product was profitable and which not, or whether there was an overall financial gain or loss. Finding out these and other facts is not only important for knowing what happened in the past year, but also to guide business decisions in the future. One who knows the mistakes of the past will avoid them in the future. Knowing which activities were successful serves as an encouragement to continue them.

Did you ever hear of "spiritual bookkeeping?"

By this we mean keeping a record of one's good deeds and *aveiros*. Few people do so. Reb Yisroel Salanter was one of those few rare individuals who did his spiritual bookkeeping in a diary where he entered — each day! — his achievements and failures. Before going to sleep, he would read his daily record. After reviewing his mistakes that day, he would express his regret and try to avoid them in the future. This, of course, is real *teshuvah*.

Reb Yisroel wanted to record his daily activities in as few words as possible. This would not only save time but also make it easier for him to review his diary at the end of each day, week, month, and year. So he adopted a highly efficient system of spiritual bookkeeping, originally developed in the book *Cheshbon Hanefesh*, a volume that he liked very much and had republished.

The *sefer* divided the human *middos* into thirteen categories. Reb Yisroel listed his own thirteen *middos* in a small pocket-size

Doing Great Things

diary, with one page per week, with spaces to record his daily performance on each *middah*. He would enter a dot in the proper box each day if he failed in one of these *middos*. If he failed more than once in the same thing, he would enter another dot, and so on. That system, involving special summary sheets for quarterly and annual periods, was very elaborate.

In order not to make it too complicated, we present here a sample chart of the weekly record, leaving out the other portions of this system of spiritual bookkeeping. We have also made the following changes: Achievements are marked by a plus and failures by a minus. The list of Reb Yisroel's thirteen *middos* appears on the following pages.

THIRTEEN MIDDOS

1
אֱמֶת
TRUTH

Do not speak before you are sure that you are telling the truth. Liars may succeed for a while, but in the long run they are not trusted or believed — even when they *do* tell the truth. Remember, your reputation depends on telling the truth.

2
זְרִיזוּת
DILIGENCE

Lose no time. Try to always keep busy doing something useful and good. Time is life — don't waste it. Be aware of your duties and obligations so that you fulfill them.

3
חֲרִיצוּת
DECISIVENESS

Train yourself to make up your mind. When you have to make a decision, do not hesitate too much. Once you have reached a decision, carry it out without delay. If you have trouble making a decision, ask for advice. Do not remain in a confused state of mind.

4
כָּבוֹד
RESPECT

Respect every human being, even if he is different, disagrees with you, or opposes you. Never forget that every human being is precious because he was created in the image of Hashem, *Tzelem Elokim*. Don't run after *kavod*, because people do not respect the arrogant. Remember the teaching of Ben Zoma: "Who is honored? He who honors others."[2]

5
מְנוּחַת הַנֶּפֶשׁ
PEACE OF MIND

Do not let little things disturb your peace of mind. Train yourself to have a "far look," which means looking ahead and thinking of the important and lasting things in life. When you do that, your mind's balance will not be upset by the small problems of daily living. Don't be in a hurry, for you may run into unexpected trouble and lose your peace of mind.

---

2 *Avos* 4:1.

6 נַחַת **GENTLENESS**		Always remember the advice of Shlomo Hamelech: "The words of the wise are spoken in quiet."[3] Speak softly and be kind to others. Even when you have a right to be angry at someone, stay in control and be kind!
7 נִקָּיוֹן **CLEANLINESS**		The Torah requires that our clothes, homes, and streets be kept clean. Our personal hygiene, or the cleanliness of our bodies, is most important. Do not cause any uncleanliness in public places.
8 סַבְלָנוּת **PATIENCE**		Everyone has some problems. It is impossible not to. Make an effort to have patience, even when you are confronted by an annoyance that you cannot avoid. When you lose your patience, your problem seems to be much more difficult than it really is. As a result, you suffer more. If your problem cannot be solved right away (like an illness, *chalilah*), why add worry and impatience to it and suffer more?
9 סֵדֶר **ORDERLINESS**		Keep everything in order and in its right place so that you will lose neither time nor patience when looking for something. Whatever you do, do it in an organized and orderly fashion. Try to concentrate on whatever you do and do not let your mind be distracted by anything else.
10 עֲנָוָה **HUMILITY**		In order to avoid conceit and to be a humble person, try to learn from all people. Every person has some knowledge or virtues that you may not have. Recognize your own shortcomings and do not overlook your friends' good qualities. No one is entitled to think that he is "the greatest." Remember, Moshe Rabbeinu, the greatest *navi*, was the most humble man ever.

---

3   *Koheles* 9:17.

11
צֶדֶק
RIGHTEOUSNESS

Remember Hillel's advice: "What is hateful to you do not do to your fellow man."[4] If you wish to be good to your fellow man, start by "giving in." The greatest source of lasting happiness is not taking away from others, but giving to them; not cheating, but helping; not looking for your own pleasure, but pleasing others. The point is to be generous, not jealous. By doing the right thing, and giving in to others, you will get along with people and your conscience will be clear.

12
קִמּוּץ
THRIFTINESS

Many people, though they have enough of everything (or may even be wealthy!), are jealous of others. Such people will never be happy. It is always good to follow Ben Zoma's teaching: "Who is rich? He who rejoices in his portion."[5]
Spend no money except to do good for yourself and others. Do not waste anything that has value. The *tzaddik* watches his money carefully because it is dear to him and kosher. "Kosher money" is money that was earned honestly. The thrifty person is economically minded, but he is not a miser. Money is to be used, not loved. Money is a means to an end; do not love it for its own sake.

13
שְׁתִיקָה
SILENCE

Many people get into trouble because they say things that should not be said. Therefore, think before you open your mouth to speak. Consider carefully what you are about to say. Ask yourself: "Will my words bring some benefit to myself or others?" If the answer is "no," or you are not sure, silence is best. Better be silent than sorry! Speech is one of man's most powerful and unique features. Some people develop a passion for talking too much, talking back, using bad language, and hurting the feelings of others by insulting them. If you want to be wise, develop a passion for silence.

---

4   *Shabbos* 31a.
5   *Avos* 4:1.

Doing Great Things

Reb Yisroel kept his daily record and taught his students to do the same. Of course, the list of the thirteen *middos* is not complete, for there are other good human qualities and their opposites. However, he felt that these thirteen are the most essential ones because they indirectly include such characteristics as peace, love, mercy, and many more.

A person's chart will show that he made some mistakes and scored some achievements. Of course, an achievement doesn't simply cancel out a mistake. Sometimes one good deed outweighs many sins and vice versa. This is where the person himself has to be the judge and, ultimately, one day he will have to answer to the Judge of all Judges, *Hakadosh Baruch Hu*.

One should not be scared and discouraged by his mistakes. We all make mistakes! Still, we should try to avoid repeating them. Neither must one become conceited by his good behavior, for there is always room for improvement.

A person seeing a written record of his good deeds will be motivated to repeat doing them. Seeing his record of failures will alert him to his shortcomings and arouse his desire and willpower to overcome them. By keeping track, we can improve and be happier, better Jews!

WEEKLY CHART FOR SPIRITUAL BOOKKEEPING

Plus signs represent achievements and minus signs represent failures.

VIRTUES	SUN.	MON.	TUE.	WED.	THUR.	FRI.	שבת
אֱמֶת TRUTH	+++ - -	++ - -	+++ - - - - -	++++ - -	++	+++ -	+++
זְרִיזוּת DILIGENCE	++	- -	+ -	+++ - -	++ - -	++ -	
חֲרִיצוּת DECISIVENESS		+ -	-	-	+	++ -	
כָּבוֹד RESPECT	-		+ -	++	++ -		+++
מְנוּחַת הַנֶּפֶשׁ PEACE OF MIND	+	- -	+ - - -	+ -	+ -		+++
נַחַת GENTLENESS	- - -	+ -	++ -	++ - -	-	++ -	+++
נְקִיוֹן CLEANLINESS	++	+	++	+	+ - -	-	+++
סַבְלָנוּת PATIENCE	-	+ - - -	++ - -	+ -	- -	+ - -	++ -
סֵדֶר ORDERLINESS	++	++	+++ -	++	+ -	++	++++ -
עֲנָוָה HUMILITY		-	+ - -		+ - -	- -	+
צֶדֶק RIGHTEOUSNESS	++	-		+ - - -		+ -	++
קִמּוּץ THRIFT	+ -	+ -	+ - -	-		+ - -	
שְׁתִיקָה SILENCE	- -	- - -	- - - - -	- - - - -	- - - -	- -	+ -

Doing Great Things

SLEEPS IN THE POORHOUSE

Poverty was widespread in the days of Reb Yisroel Salanter. There was no government help to the poor, no health insurance, and no unemployment benefits. Those who were very poor used to go begging from *shtetl* to *shtetl* and from house to house. They had little choice.

Jews, of course, took care of their poor as best they could, in keeping with the great tradition of *tzedakah*. Though most of the Jews who suffered from economic restrictions imposed by the Czarist authorities were impoverished, they would share their bread with the poor.

Each town or *shtetl* used to have a poorhouse, known as the *hekdesh*. The *hekdesh* also served as a kind of inn for the traveling poor. There they would find a place to sleep and rest and sometimes even a meal.

When Reb Yisroel came to Kovno, he inspected the poorhouse and found that the building and furniture had deteriorated, causing much hardship to the poor travelers. The roof was leaking; the walls were unpainted and had many cracks; windows were broken; and the furniture was falling apart. He appealed to the leader of the *kehillah* to repair the *hekdesh*. He was told that these repairs would cost much money and that the community had no funds on hand.

Reb Yisroel did not agree with these leaders. He argued that this is not the way to observe the great mitzvah of *hachnasas orchim*, taking care of wayfarers. Seeing that the leaders of the Kovno community took no action, Reb Yisroel decided to do something dramatic: he went to sleep in the poorhouse!

The next morning, the news spread rapidly in Kovno. People were asking each other: "Why does this great *tzaddik* sleep in

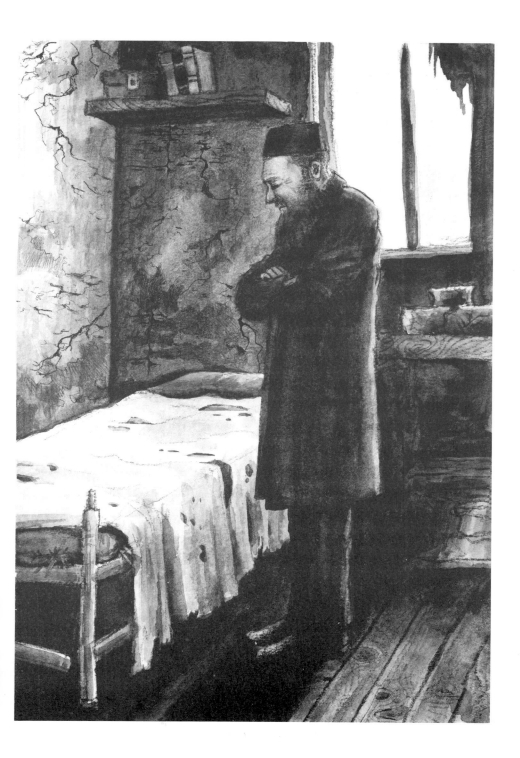

the *hekdesh*?" A large crowd gathered around the poorhouse and asked him why he spent the night there. He answered and warned them: "I will continue sleeping here with the poor people until the *kehillah* repairs this dilapidated building. The poor are entitled to a decent place for lodging." The crowd shouted its consent: "Reb Yisroel is right. The *hekdesh* must be fixed!"

The leadership of the Kovno Jewish community now felt ashamed. They immediately set out to make a special collection. When enough money was raised, Reb Yisroel left the poorhouse. The repairs began at once and the *hekdesh* was remodeled.

HOSPITALITY

People usually think that the mitzvah of *hachnasas orchim*, hospitality, applies only to such cases when guests show up on their own. Reb Yisroel extended this mitzvah further: he went to seek out those who might be *potential* guests. If there was a visitor in town, or a poor individual who was too embarrassed to ask for a place to lodge or eat, Reb Yisroel would invite him to his house. Sometimes he would bring food or money to that person's house if the guest did not want to leave home.

Reb Yisroel did not wait for the poor to come to him; he went to them first.

He was very sensitive to the needs of the poor, the widow, the orphan, and the wayfarer. He was also sensitive to the rights and dignity of the poor. If someone dared to insult a beggar, Reb Yisroel would rebuke him. Sometimes, people who resented the ever-increasing stream of beggars knocking at their doors would call them "parasites" or "no-goodniks." Reb Yisroel did not approve of this sort of talk. He would deliver special *drashos* on the mitzvah of receiving guests properly and respectfully. He would criticize the wealthy who lived in luxury and hesitated to give handouts to the poor.

When he lived in Salant, he studied in a secluded place day and night. His in-laws used to send him coffee and a pastry for breakfast each morning. Knowing that in the adjoining shul there were several poor old men, Reb Yisroel would persuade the daily messenger to give the pastry to the old men. He told the young messenger: "Those unfortunate poor old men can't even chew the stale bread they are given by the community. Go and exchange these fresh soft cakes for their bread. I am young and can eat the bread, but they are old and have no teeth, so they need something soft to eat." The messenger boy was further told by Reb Yisroel not to reveal his secret. For many years, he exchanged his fresh pastry for the stale bread of the poor.

When Reb Yisroel would come to shul on Yom Kippur, he would bring some food along. He explained it this way: "If, G-d forbid, someone should faint, it will be necessary to feed him. Let me have the food ready. This may save a life."

Of course, receiving guests does not only apply to food. Sometimes a few cheerful words of encouragement are even more important. Whenever guests came to his home, Reb Yisroel would behave toward each one in a different way. "People are different in so many ways," he said. "You can't treat them the same way. Some individuals must be served food immediately, while others must first be engaged in conversation. It is most important to know how to please each guest."

When Reb Yisroel lived in Kovno, the well-known rabbi of Lomzha, Rabbi Binyamin Diskin, visited the city. All the *talmidei chachamim* of Kovno, including Reb Yisroel, came to visit him. The scholars engaged the learned visitor in a lively Torah discussion that lasted until after midnight. The guest, being tired and hungry, remarked that he would like to eat something. Quietly Reb Yisroel slipped out of the room, and before anyone had time to do anything for the guest, he returned carrying a tray filled with food for the visiting rabbi. Like Avraham Avinu, Reb Yisroel performed the mitzvah of hospitality by himself, not through messengers.

KOL NIDRE

It was the eve of Yom Kippur. The people of Salant had gathered in the shul. The men wrapped themselves in their *talleisim* and were ready for the introductory prayer of *Kol Nidre*. It was getting late, but the *tefillah* had not yet begun because Reb Yisroel had not arrived as yet.

When it became too late to delay *Kol Nidre* any further, it was decided to start *davening*. *Kol Nidre* was concluded and Reb Yisroel still had not come. It was decided to wait for him before beginning *Maariv*.

It was very dark outside and still Reb Yisroel was not there. The people began worrying about him. After all, he never came late to shul — especially on Yom Kippur. His wife, who was in shul, didn't know what had happened to her husband and became alarmed. They sent someone to run to his home, but he was not there.

When *Maariv* was almost finished, Reb Yisroel entered the shul. His clothes, which were always clean and neat, looked

wrinkled and his beautiful beard disheveled. The community waited until he had finished *davening* and then asked him what had happened to him. He told them the following story:

"As I walked to shul, I heard a baby crying hysterically in one of the houses nearby. I knocked and there was no answer. The baby kept crying, so I entered the house. The baby must have been very hungry because it stopped crying as soon as I fed him some milk. His little six-year-old sister, who was the babysitter, had fallen asleep and did not hear the baby crying. I fed the baby, comforted him, and put him to sleep. As I was getting ready to leave, the six-year-old woke up. She begged me not to leave because she was afraid to be alone at home with the baby. She told me that her mother had gone to shul for *Kol Nidre*, so I remained and said *Kol Nidre* in their home." Reb Yisroel added. "You see my clothes and my beard, how wrinkled and disorderly they are. The baby had a good time playing with my beard," he smiled.

Reb Yisroel said that he was very happy to have performed such a great mitzvah on the holy night of Yom Kippur. Helping those two children was more important than *davening* in shul on Yom Kippur.

PREVENTING A SUICIDE

When Reb Yisroel lived in Zarece, a suburb of Vilna, he attracted a large number of students to his yeshiva. Each day, he would deliver a *shiur* at an appointed time. Being a very punctual man, he would always come to the yeshiva on time.

One morning, as the Beis Hamedrash was filled to capacity with an eager crowd of students and outsiders waiting to hear one of his brilliant lectures, the master did not show up. After an hour of impatient waiting, it was decided to send several students to his home. He was not home. The students, now worried, began searching the neighborhood. As they reached a local bridge, they noticed Reb Yisroel standing by the bank of the river speaking to a young woman. The students, thinking that this must be a serious or private matter, did not wish to disturb their master and returned to the yeshiva.

Finally, Reb Yisroel came to the yeshiva. He apologized for being late, due to a most serious matter involving *pikuach nefesh*, and proceeded to deliver his *shiur*. After the *shiur*, he was questioned by his students as to the reason for his delay. He told them the following:

> As I crossed the bridge this morning on my way to the yeshiva, I saw a young woman running toward the river. She appeared distressed and disheveled. I stopped her and asked her why she was running so fast and if I could be of any help. The woman, who seemed very troubled, told me to mind my own business and started running again toward the river. Fearing for her safety, I gave chase, grabbed her by her hand, and insisted that she tell the reason for her strange behavior.
>
> The woman began crying hysterically. After I calmed her, she told me her tragic story. Her two children had recently died. Her husband, the family's only breadwinner, had collapsed at the children's funeral and had been ill ever since. Her husband — who was a horse and buggy driver, a *baal agalah* — had to hire another man to substitute

Doing Great Things **55**

for him. Though they now earned much less, it was enough to support her husband and herself and pay the doctor bills. But yesterday their horse died. "This was the final blow," said the woman. "We have no more income, no more hope. I cannot go on suffering any longer. I decided to commit suicide by drowning in the river."

I talked to her for a long time. I told her, "You must never give up hope. Hashem will hear your cry and answer your prayers. You are still young. You will give birth again and have *nachas* from your new children. Your husband will recover soon. As to a horse, I *promise* you that by tomorrow I will bring you enough money to buy a new one."

Slowly, the woman calmed down. She thanked me for saving her life and being so kind. She then returned home to care for her sick husband.

TELLING JOKES

Reb Yisroel Salanter was usually a serious man. He was always mindful of the important things in life, like our duties and responsibilities to Hashem and to men. The suffering of the Jews in Russia, the lack of real Yiddishkeit in many Jewish communities, the threat to Orthodoxy from various nonreligious groups, and many other serious matters concerned him greatly.

He was also a man of few words. He spoke slowly and carefully, watching each word so that it did not offend anyone or contain any exaggeration.

No one expected to see him talking much, let alone telling jokes and laughing!

Yet, one day his students saw him standing in a Vilna street talking to a certain man for quite some time. He told the man many jokes and funny stories. This unusual scene attracted much attention from passersby, who looked on with amazement.

The following day, one of his students said to him: "Rebbe, many of us cannot understand why you spent so much time talking, laughing, and telling jokes."

Reb Yisroel replied: "The man I was talking to was a troubled man. He faced many problems and was very depressed. I thought it was a real mitzvah to cheer him up. The act of *gemilus chassadim*, doing kindness, does not always have to involve the giving of money; cheering up an unhappy man is no less important."

HELPING SAVE THE JEWS OF KOVNO

In the year 1869, there was a serious shortage of food in Lithuania due to a drought. Rabbi Yitzchok Elchonon, Chief Rabbi of Kovno, decided that under such conditions it is permissible to eat *kitniyos* on Pesach.

You probably know that Ashkenazi Jews do not eat certain foods on Pesach called *kitniyos*. The forbidden foods include rice, beans, peas, corn, and the like. These foods are not really *chametz*, but many centuries ago European Jews had adopted this *minhag*.

The Chief Rabbi of Kovno therefore reasoned that when hunger threatens the Jewish community it is permissible to eat *kitniyos*. When Reb Yitzchok Elchonon consulted some rabbis, they opposed his decision. Some even protested publicly.

Reb Yitzchok Elchonon now turned to Reb Yisroel Salanter to join him in issuing the official permission, or *heter*, to eat *kitniyos* on Pesach. The Chief Rabbi informed him that even his own family would be eating *kitniyos* that Pesach. Reb Yisroel immediately agreed and the *heter* of the Chief Rabbi of Kovno was issued. On Pesach of 5629 (1869), the Jews of Kovno ate *kitniyos*. They did not have enough *matzah* or any other food. If they would not have been permitted to eat the above-mentioned foods, many of them would have starved.

UNUSUAL AID

The train from Kovno to Vilna was crowded and noisy. In one of the cars there sat a young man who looked nervous, irritated, and angry. Almost all of the passengers smoked cigarettes or pipes, as this car was reserved for smokers (in those days, they didn't know how dangerous smoking was). The young man, who did not smoke, did not seem to mind the smoking. But when an older, quiet-looking man who sat across from him lit up a cigarette, the young fellow started ridiculing and insulting him. It seemed that whatever the old man did, the young one found fault with him.

The young man, turning angrily to the older one, protested: "You are filling the air with smoke. It is impossible to breathe here because of your smoking!" The older gentleman put out his cigarette and politely apologized: "I am sorry. I didn't know that you would mind my smoking."

A few minutes later, the angry young person shouted again

at the old man: "Close that window! Do I have to freeze here because you like to keep the window open?" The old man rose, closed the window, and again apologized: "I beg your pardon, sir. I merely opened the window for a while to clear the air. I thought you would appreciate this." "Do me no favors!" cried the angry young fellow.

The train pulled up at the Vilna station. A large group of Jews, including some distinguished rabbis, was waiting there. As soon as the older gentleman stepped off the train, the waiting crowd welcomed him warmly. Cries of "*Shalom aleichem*, Reb Yisroel Salanter!" were heard from all sides. The people looked at Reb Yisroel with affection and admiration. Everyone tried to shake hands with the great visitor.

The young brash fellow, realizing that he had insulted one of the saintliest of men for no real reason, felt deeply ashamed. He left the railroad station in a hurry. When he came to his hotel he was so upset that he couldn't sleep all night. In the morning, he decided to visit Reb Yisroel and beg forgiveness.

When the young man entered Reb Yisroel's hotel room, he was greeted warmly. Before he had a chance to extend his apologies, Reb Yisroel invited him to sit down. In a very friendly manner, he asked the young man: "Did you have a chance to rest after the lengthy and tiring train ride?"

The young offender couldn't say a word. He wept bitterly as he asked Reb Yisroel to forgive his terrible conduct. Reb Yisroel assured him that he forgave him. "One learns best through mistakes. I am sure that you will not do this again to anyone," he said.

Reb Yisroel then asked his visitor why he had come to Vilna. "I came here to obtain a certificate, *kabbalah*, to become a *shochet*," he answered. Reb Yisroel promised to help him and personally introduced the young man to those who were scheduled to give him the necessary examination.

Unfortunately, the young candidate failed in his test; he simply did not know the laws of *shechitah* well enough. Reb Yisroel came to his rescue. He arranged with a prominent *shochet* to teach the young candidate. Moreover, since the young man was poor, Reb Yisroel obtained some money to support him as long as he had to remain studying in Vilna.

Finally, the young man became a *shochet*. He came to say goodbye to Reb Yisroel and to thank him for his kindness. He said that he must ask the following question: "I know that you are a *tzaddik*, so I wasn't surprised when you forgave me for having insulted you. But I don't understand why you have taken such an interest in me and given me so much help. After all, I didn't deserve all of this kindness. I am sure that no one else would have done so much for me. Why did you do it?"

Reb Yisroel replied: "When I said that I forgive you, I wasn't yet sure whether I had fully forgiven you. I was worried that perhaps deep in my heart I may still resent you for what you had done to me on the train. I therefore decided to do you some favors as the best way of getting to like you. I am convinced that when people help each other, they become real friends. Taking an interest in you brought me closer to you, and as a result whatever resentment I had completely disappeared."

A YOUNG ORPHAN

The Russian king, Czar Nicholas the First, was an enemy of the Jewish people. He wanted to force the Jews of Russia to convert to the Russian Orthodox Church. As the Jews did not show the slightest inclination to give up their religion, the Czar decided to force the Jews of Russia to become Christians.

How was he to achieve his evil goal? In 1827, he issued a law to draft many Jews into the Russian army at a very young age. Non-Jews were drafted at the age of eighteen, and they would serve only a few years. The Jews, however, would now be drafted at the age of twelve! Furthermore, Jewish soldiers would have to serve *thirty years* in the Russian army!

This new law spread terror through the Jewish communities of Russia. Parents of young boys were stricken with panic. Many tried to hide their young sons. But the police, who conducted an intensive search, would usually find them and simply kidnap the children. Many mothers who cried hysterically as they embraced their precious sons were savagely beaten by the cruel police.

The young boys were taken to faraway cities where no Jews lived, sometimes as far as Siberia. They were placed in military training schools, called Cantons. The young Jewish soldiers were therefore called Cantonists. Sometimes, the young captives would be placed in a private gentile home. In either case, the boys were forced to eat nonkosher food, work on Shabbos, go to Church on Sundays, kiss the cross, and act as "good Christians."

Most of the young Jewish boys who were taken refused to be forced into Christianity. Their sadistic military superiors did everything they could to break down the faith of the Jewish children. Those who refused to kiss the cross or eat ham would be beaten mercilessly, denied food, and forced to spend nights outside in the bitter, subzero weather of Siberia.

As a result, many Jewish Cantonists died during the early years of their military training, and some became disabled. Of those who survived, some became loyal Christians, some forgot their Jewish origins, while others somehow managed to remain faithful to Judaism.

Reb Yisroel Salanter was terribly upset by this inhuman treatment of Jewish children. He used to say: "This evil decree breaks my heart and may shorten my life."

He organized a special committee consisting of his loyal *talmidim* and followers to seek the repeal of this unjust draft law. He sent delegates, known as *shtadlonim*, to St. Petersburg, which was then the capital city of Russia, to meet with high government officials. He was also among the leaders of special emergency meetings of Russian rabbis where this problem was discussed.

The law did not call for the drafting of every Jewish boy. Each Jewish community would receive an order to supply a certain number of Cantonists. This led to additional injustices. The rich families would bribe the police so that it was poor boys who would usually be caught and sent away. Sometimes the leaders of a *shtetl* were forced by the rich to select children of poor families.

Once, when Reb Yisroel lived in Kovno, a poor mother, whose son was kidnapped to become a Cantonist, entered the shul during Shabbos *davening* shouting her protest and weeping bitterly. It was customary in European communities for someone who had a claim or a grievance to halt the *davening*. This was called *ikuv hakriah*, stopping the reading of the Torah. The person who came to state his complaint publicly stood in front of the *Aron Hakodesh* and simply did not let anyone take

Doing Great Things

the Torah out. Of course, no one would want to fight in front of the *Aron*, so the person who was wronged had a good chance to ask for the community's help. In most cases, this method worked well.

But when the grieved mother approached the *Aron* screaming and crying, several men (probably the rich ones who did not want their sons to go to the army) ran up toward the poor lady and began pushing her away from the *Aron*. Reb Yisroel came to the woman's rescue. He scolded those who had the chutzpah to embarrass the unfortunate mother. He said to them: "Such people like you have stone hearts." The men pulled back in shame. The woman pleaded with the congregation and then left the shul. After the Torah was finally taken from the *Aron*, Reb Yisroel left the shul saying: "When such cruelty occurs publicly in a shul, one is not allowed to *daven* here."

There was another case regarding a Cantonist in which Reb Yisroel became seriously involved, showing the kindness of his sensitive soul and his hatred of unfairness and cruelty.

The town of Salant received an order to deliver one young boy to the army. Each family, and every young boy, was now worried as everyone wondered who the victim might be.

One day, a poor widow and her young son came to town. The woman carried a music box, *katarinka* in Russian. The poor widow, who had no home and no income, would play her music on street corners and in the market place. People would stop, listen to her sad music, shake their heads, and drop a few coins in a box carried by the pale-looking orphan.

The leaders of the community, who were still looking for a victim, decided that this orphan would be the right candidate. They seized the little orphan, changed his name, and gave him a local address and registered him with the police as a candidate for the army. The shocked mother cried hysterically. She ran from house to house looking for her only child. She pleaded with everyone to return her son to her but no one listened. The troubled woman stopped eating and drinking, tore her hair, and almost became insane.

Reb Yisroel, who had moved from Salant a long time before, had just returned for a visit. The widow, who didn't know him, saw him in the street, saw his distinguished appearance, and hoped that he might be able to help. She walked over to him and told him of her tragedy. He listened very attentively and an expression of sadness covered his face. He calmed her and told her to come to see him after Shabbos.

Shabbos came. Reb Yisroel went to shul. He didn't talk to anyone about the young orphan. Shabbos morning after *davening*, there was a *Kiddush* in his honor arranged by the community leaders. All the important people of the town came to the *Kiddush*, held at the inn where Reb Yisroel was staying.

Kiddush was recited. Food was served. Everyone inquired about Reb Yisroel's health and family. People wanted to hear from Reb Yisroel, who by now was a famous Rav and traveler, how Jews were getting along in other communities.

Suddenly Reb Yisroel rose from his place. The people fell silent. Everyone anticipated hearing a learned *shiur* on the weekly *parshah*, and a report on the state of the Jewish people. But this time, the gentle Reb Yisroel had a different lecture in mind.

He began criticizing the leaders of Salant for kidnapping the orphan boy for the army. His voice grew louder, and with righteous indignation he shouted at the astonished people: "You are murderers! You are kidnappers!"

He then turned to various individuals whom he had known for so many years. "You, Reb Chaim," he cried, "consider yourself a real *tzaddik*. You take so much pride in your strict observance of Shabbos. How dare you violate the Torah's law against kidnapping, which is punishable by death?"

"And you, Reb Mendel," he shouted, "You are so careful in observing *mitzvos*, but you don't seem to worry about turning over a Jewish child, an orphan, to *shmad*, conversion."

"And you, Reb Yaakov," he screamed, "You always buy the most beautiful *esrog* in town because you are so religious. How could you violate the law forbidding the oppression of a widow and an orphan?"

Reb Yisroel kept on rebuking all the other leaders, one by one. The people were so shocked and bewildered that no one made a sound. He finally declared that he did not intend to remain in the company of such criminals and ran out of the inn.

This incident became known immediately all throughout Salant. The ordinary citizens, who were not involved in this scandal, agreed with him. Many people were saying: "Yes, the rabbi is right. Jews should never be guilty of kidnapping, especially an orphan."

Even the guilty community leaders were now sorry. After hearing Reb Yisroel's harsh accusations they realized that they had committed a terrible sin. They decided to return the orphan to his mother. But, so ashamed were they, and so afraid of Reb Yisroel, that they simply had no courage to face him, even to announce their good decision.

One of Reb Yisroel's *talmidim*, Rabbi Eliyohu of Kartinga, was asked to go to Reb Yisroel and inform him that the boy will be freed. But Reb Yisroel was nowhere to be found. After a

lengthy search, Rabbi Eliyohu found his master outside of the town, sitting on a rock muttering to himself: "Woe unto me that my people should be guilty of such terrible sins. Woe unto me that it happened in my own town of Salant."

Reb Yisroel agreed to return to Salant only after his trusted *talmid* assured him that the young orphan would be freed and returned to his mother.

Years later, when the evil draft law was finally repealed, Reb Yisroel recited a special *brachah* of thanksgiving, *Hatov Vehametiv*. He said: "This day is like a holiday. It is a day of rejoicing."

- Chapter Three -

LITTLE THINGS COUNT TOO

RABBI YEHUDAH HANASI USED TO SAY: "Be careful to observe an easy mitzvah as you would a difficult one, for you do not know the reward for each mitzvah."[6] Reb Yisroel took this advice seriously. He observed each mitzvah meticulously and his saintliness shone through all of his actions, great or small. The stories in this chapter are shorter and seem to involve "less important" things. But to Reb Yisroel, every mitzvah and every situation was important.

EATING DAYS

Thankfully, few Jewish children in America today go to sleep hungry. Most Jewish children live in comfortable homes, wear fine clothes, eat good food, and receive proper medical care.

Jewish children in nineteenth-century Russia and Lithuania did not have it so good. Most of them were poor, lacking food,

---

6   *Avos* 2:1.

medical care, clothing, and decent housing. Many yeshiva students would sleep on hard benches in the yeshiva. When Reb Yisroel came to Kovno, he visited the yeshivos. He became unhappy about the living conditions of the yeshiva students. The yeshivos had no money to provide food. Some of the boys who came from out of town had no money to buy their own food. Each day of the week they used to eat in someone else's home. This practice was known as *essen teg*, eating days. Each *zman* (semester), the boy would eat on Sundays with one family, on Mondays with another, etc. Reb Yisroel Salanter thought that it was not dignified for students studying Torah in a yeshiva to eat each day at someone else's table. As a matter of fact, the students too were unhappy. Yet those poor boys had no choice.

So Reb Yisroel decided to make a "revolution" in Kovno. Instead of inviting a poor scholar, each family would contribute a certain amount to a special fund. The students would stop eating at the homes of different families, and instead eat in a dining room to be created at their own yeshiva. This of course raised the students' spirits. Naturally, they did better in their studies too. A student who is respected and happy is usually a better student.

SLEEPLESS NIGHTS

Reb Yisroel had some favorite sayings, selected from the Torah or *Chazal* (our Sages). For days (or weeks!) he would repeat a particular saying. Then he would choose a new saying and concentrate on it in the same manner. Old sayings were not forgotten; he would come back to them from time to time.

The rabbi of Russia's capital city of St. Petersburg, Rabbi Yitzchok Blazer, who was one of the important *talmidim* of Reb Yisroel Salanter, wrote: "My great rebbe, *zt"l*, used to study *mussar* with great feeling and joy. Sometimes, he would repeat a certain saying many times. Quite often, he would have tears in his eyes as he would concentrate on a chosen saying."

The saintly Rabbi Yisroel Meir Hakohen of Radin, known as the Chofetz Chaim, once stayed in the same hotel with Reb Yisroel and reported the following: "I had the *zechus* (privilege) of being close to the great *tzaddik*, Reb Yisroel Salanter. Since my room was adjoining his, I was curious to know what this great man does at night. During the quiet of the night, when all guests were asleep, I heard him repeat over and over the saying of Hillel: 'He who does not learn deserves to die.'"[7] The Chofetz Chaim reported that he heard Reb Yisroel crying and learning all night, and he could tell that Reb Yisroel did so quietly so as not to disturb the other guests.

Many other people who observed Reb Yisroel reported that he had many such sleepless nights.

Some people have sleepless nights because they can't sleep.

Reb Yisroel didn't sleep many nights because he didn't always want to sleep.

AS LONG AS THE CANDLE BURNS

In the poverty-stricken areas of Russia, only the rich had more than one pair of shoes. The poor were glad to have one pair — for some of them had none at all! Reb Yisroel, who had chosen a life of poverty, had a single pair of shoes. When the

---

[7] *Avos* 1:13.

shoes had to be repaired, he would go to the shoemaker and wait until the shoes were fixed.

One evening, Reb Yisroel walked into the shoemaker's shop and asked: "I would like to have my shoes fixed, but I am worried that it's too late. I don't want you to work late because of me. Shall I come back tomorrow?" "No," replied the shoemaker. "It's not too late. Please sit down."

Of course, there were no electric lights in those days. The shoemaker was so poor that he couldn't even afford a kerosene lamp. All he had was a candle, most of which was already consumed.

The shoemaker, pointing at the candle, turned to him and said: "You see, Rebbe, as long as the candle burns, one can still do some mending." This innocent statement struck a responsive chord in the sensitive heart of Reb Yisroel Salanter, for to him the shoemaker's words had a very special meaning.

For weeks Reb Yisroel kept on saying: "The soul we have received from Hashem is like a candle; it burns for a limited time only. As long as this candle burns, we can still improve our ways."

10,000 RUBLES FOR 5,000?

Many religious people say that they have *bitachon* (trust) in Hashem. This means that a person recognizes that all that he has and whatever happens to him comes from Hashem.

Once, after Reb Yisroel had delivered a lengthy speech on the importance of *bitachon*, a simple-minded laborer walked over to him and asked: "Rebbe, please tell me, if I have complete trust in Hashem, will He grant my request?" "Yes," replied Reb

Yisroel. "Suppose I will ask for 10,000 rubles," asked the laborer, "will He give it to me?" "He will, if you have real *bitachon*," replied Reb Yisroel.

The man was happy. He returned home and said to his wife: "We will soon get rich. Reb Yisroel himself promised me that I will have 10,000 rubles." As a result, this laborer stopped working. He sat home, doing nothing, awaiting the miraculous arrival of the expected treasure. Weeks went by and there was no sign of any treasure. The family, having used up its meager savings, was now on the brink of starvation. The wife urged her husband to see Reb Yisroel. "After all, he *promised* you 10,000 rubles," said the wife.

The man came to Reb Yisroel and complained: "Rebbe, you promised me 10,000 rubles. Why wasn't your promise fulfilled? I want you to know that my family is starving. We must have the money immediately."

Reb Yisroel nodded his head sympathetically. He quietly told the man: "A person who *really* trusts in Hashem will certainly get his wish granted. However, if you have no patience, I have an offer to make. I happen to have 5,000 rubles with me. Are you ready to trade your expected 10,000 rubles for the 5,000 right now?" The man's eyes lit up. "Of course, Rebbe, I'll be glad to take your 5,000!" the man exclaimed.

"I am afraid," said Reb Yisroel, "that you *do not* have real *bitachon* in Hashem. If you would *really* have *bitachon*, how do you give away 10,000 rubles for 5,000?" he asked. "Go back to work and stop deceiving yourself. You will not get the 10,000 rubles because your trust in Hashem is not yet complete. Only those who put their full trust in Hashem deserve and receive His help," he concluded.

SERVING HIS SHAMASH

Once, Reb Yisroel became ill and had to travel to Germany to see a well-known doctor. His students appointed an elderly man to accompany their master and serve as his *shamash*. The old man, a lonely and quiet person, felt very honored to be the attendant of such a great man.

During the journey, the *shamash* took sick. Reb Yisroel took care of him and provided all of his needs. The *shamash* was unhappy. "Rebbe," he said to Reb Yisroel, "Woe to me that I, a simple man, should be served by you, the leader of our generation."

The *shamash* pleaded, "Please, Rebbe, do not serve me. I don't think it's right."

But Reb Yisroel replied that he must not and will not give up the mitzvah of *bikur cholim*, caring for the sick, and he continued attending to his sick *shamash*. In order to make the old man feel comfortable, Reb Yisroel told him, "The ways of Hashem are hidden from man. It was decreed that you should be ill. However, since you are lonely no one would have come to your aid. So Hashem decided to make me sick and have you accompany me. Now that you are with me and I take care of you, it is quite possible that Hashem will take away my illness. So you see, by helping you I am really helping myself too."

THE "MIXED-UP" SHIUR

When Reb Yisroel would come to a city, he would always be invited to give a *shiur*. Before he would deliver his lecture, he would post an announcement on the shul's bulletin board indicating the topic of the *shiur* and the various sources he would discuss. This was very helpful to his audience, for they would study the selections very carefully and be ready for the *shiur*. His lectures were so advanced and complicated that even scholars had difficulty following them. Preparing for the *shiur* was therefore a must for everyone who wanted to understand.

Once, someone played a prank on him. The announcement Reb Yisroel posted, containing more than one hundred sources, was removed and another one put in its place. The new announcement contained a random listing of unrelated topics and selections. The purpose of this prank was to embarrass Reb Yisroel in public.

The next day, when he walked up to the *bimah* to deliver the *shiur*, he asked to see the announcement that had been posted. When he took one look at the paper, he turned pale. He stood there, deep in thought, for a full ten minutes. The audience, unaware of what happened, was worried about him. "Maybe he doesn't feel well," someone whispered.

But then he began lecturing. His lecture was so brilliant and interesting that everyone gasped in amazement.

After the *shiur*, two young students came to him and apologized. "We played this trick on you," they said, "to test your scholarship. We now see that you are a *gaon* of the highest order. Please forgive us." And of course he did.

When Rabbi Naftoli Amsterdam, one of Reb Yisroel's trusted followers, used to tell this story he would say: "Such a genius didn't need ten minutes to create a new *shiur*. The reason he waited so long was that he debated with himself whether it was proper to go ahead with the new lecture. He was afraid that he might appear as a 'show off,' which he never liked."

A GOOD JEW?

When a *chassid* visits his Rebbe, he usually asks the Rebbe for a *brachah*. The request is written down on a piece of paper, called a *kvittel*, and handed to the Rebbe. The *chassid* also presents the Rebbe with a gift of money called a *pidyon*. In Lithuania, a great *tzaddik* was affectionately called a *Guter Yid*, a Good Jew, and some people would come to him for a *brachah*. However, Lithuanian Jews did not develop the custom of giving the *tzaddik* either a *kvittel* or a *pidyon*.

Once, a *chassid* came to Lithuania. He heard that Reb Yisroel Salanter is the *Guter Yid* of the Lithuanian Jews and decided to visit him.

After having talked to Reb Yisroel for a while, the *chassid* put down his *kvittel* on the table and one hundred rubles of *pidyon* money. Reb Yisroel did not make any comment. The *chassid* thought that perhaps in Lithuania it was not proper to give a "mere" one hundred rubles to a *Guter Yid*, so he added another hundred rubles. Reb Yisroel still made no move. The *chassid* was confused. "Are Lithuanian *tzaddikim* so expensive?" he thought. So he took out 500 rubles, a very large sum of money in those days, and placed them before Reb Yisroel.

Reb Yisroel finally asked, "Why did you put so much money on my table?" "Well," replied the *chassid*, "it is our custom to give *piydon* to the *Guter Yid* when we ask for his *brachah*." Reb Yisroel smiled, told the *chassid* to take back his money, and said to him: "In Lithuania, we consider one as a *Guter Yid* if he gives away his money to others. Since you are ready to give so much, you are the real *Guter Yid*. Would you, then, please give me your *brachah*?"

A CAT FOR YOM KIPPUR

It was Erev Yom Kippur. The Jews of Salant were getting ready for the holy day. What a strange sight it must have been to see Reb Yisroel coaxing a cat to enter his house.

Someone asked: "Rebbe, didn't you teach us that Erev Yom Kippur is a day of preparation for the holy day of Yom Kippur, and that we should spend all of our time doing *teshuvah*? So why do you waste time on a cat today?"

Replied Reb Yisroel: "I have borrowed several *sefarim*. Since we have mice in our house, I fear that on Yom Kippur, when no one is home, the mice might damage those *sefarim* and I would then be guilty of negligence. Do you now understand why I need a cat for Yom Kippur?" he asked.

THE WATER CARRIER

Reb Yisroel was once invited to eat in the house of his friend, Reb Yaakov Karpas in Kovno. Before dinner was served, every member of the family washed his hands, as required, using much water. Reb Yisroel, however, washed his hands with a minimum of water.

Since it is preferable to wash with much water, the host asked him: "We have plenty of water in the house, why don't you take some more?" Reb Yisroel replied: "Because your house stands on a hill." Reb Yaakov was now really puzzled. "What does this have to do with the water?" he asked. "Think of the water carrier," Reb Yisroel replied. His host still didn't understand.

"I noticed," said Reb Yisroel, "that your maid has to carry pails of water from the well that is down the hill. Carrying two full pails of water uphill to your house is a very difficult job. If

I would use more water, you might run out of water and your maid would have to carry two more heavy pails. I have to wash my hands because it is required by *halachah*. However, I have no right to use more than the minimum requirement if this will result in an extra hardship or burden on someone else."

"DON'T STAND IN THE DOORWAY!"

The Kovno region had suffered unseasonal hot and humid weather for several weeks, and there was no relief in sight. Rosh Hashanah came and the shuls were packed with people. In those pre-air-conditioning days, the heat in the shul where Reb Yisroel *davened* was unbearable. Every seat was taken and some people were standing. The crowds came to listen to Reb Yisroel's outstanding *drashos*.

After he delivered a very stirring speech, the *tefillos* continued. One of his *talmidim*, who must have looked for a little fresh air, placed himself in the open doorway.

Reb Yisroel walked up to that *talmid* and reprimanded him: "You robber! Don't stand in the doorway. By blocking the doorway you stop the outside air from coming into the shul. Should someone in the shul faint because of lack of fresh air, you will be guilty of contributing to it. It is hot enough as it is. Don't rob the people of their air."

A SHORT SHEMONEH ESREI

Reb Yisroel once visited the famous Gerer Rebbe, Rabbi Yitzchak Meir Alter. The Rebbe was very pleased with his visitor and received him with great honors. The Gerer *chassidim*, upon hearing that their Rebbe had a distinguished guest, crowded into the shul where Reb Yisroel came to *daven Minchah*.

Many *tzaddikim* are accustomed to *daven* a long *Shemoneh Esrei*. The *chassidim*, having heard by now that Reb Yisroel Salanter was the great Lithuanian *tzaddik*, expected that his *Shemoneh Esrei* would take quite some time. They were in for a disappointment, though — his *Shemoneh Esrei* was finished practically in no time, as if he were an ordinary, simple Jew! The *chassidim* couldn't understand what happened and simply stared in amazement.

Reb Yisroel understood their puzzlement and thought that an explanation was in order. "Gentlemen," he said, turning to the *chassidim*, "I noticed that many of you have given up your work or business because you wanted to see me. This is an ordinary working day. I know that most of you cannot afford to leave your work. If I would *daven Shemoneh Esrei* for a long time, I would have caused you a financial loss. If I want to *daven* a long *Shemoneh Esrei,* I'll do it on my own time — not at your expense."

A QUICK SHABBOS MEAL

Once, Reb Yisroel was invited by one of his *talmidim* for a Shabbos meal. Reb Yisroel told his *talmid* that before he accepts the invitation he must ask him some questions. He wanted to know how the Shabbos meal is conducted. The *talmid*, a rich man, explained in detail how elaborate his Shabbos meals are. The meat, purchased from a highly reliable kosher butcher, is one-hundred percent *glatt* kosher without any doubts. The cook, a widow, is a very religious and dependable woman.

Little Things Count Too **79**

During the Friday night meal, *zemiros* are sung and Torah is studied so that the meal is finished at a very late hour.

The *talmid* must have been surprised when his Rebbe told him that he would accept his invitation on condition that the Friday night meal would be finished at an earlier hour. The *talmid* agreed, considering it a great honor to have his Rebbe as his guest.

Friday night during the meal, Reb Yisroel refrained from any lengthy conversation, even concerning Torah study. Much before the regular ending time, he requested that the *birchas hamazon* be recited. The host agreed but asked: "Rebbe, please tell me, did you find anything wrong in my house that you are in such a hurry to leave?"

Reb Yisroel did not reply. Instead, he turned to the cook and said to her: "I beg your pardon, madam, for rushing you so much this evening. This must have tired you out." The widow replied: "No, Rebbe, quite to the contrary. I wish to thank *you* for getting my work finished early. I am always very tired on Friday nights after a long day's work. Tonight, I am going home early, thanks to you. We should have more guests like you!"

After the cook left, Reb Yisroel said to his host: "You now have the answer to your question. It is certainly nice to conduct a lengthy Shabbos meal. However, you may not do so at the expense of a tired woman, especially a widow who must be given special treatment."

YAHRZEIT KADDISH

When Reb Yisroel visited the German city of Memel, he came to the shul on the day of his father's *yahrzeit* to

say *Kaddish*. In many communities, it is the custom that the *yahrzeit Kaddish*, recited after *Aleinu*, should be said by one person only. The *shamash* announced that because Reb Yisroel was observing his father's *yahrzeit* today, he alone was to say the *Kaddish*.

Just before *davening* began, an average Jew named Yitzchak Isaacsohn entered the shul. He turned to the *shamash* and said: "I am observing my daughter's *yahrzeit* today, so let me say the *Kaddish* after *Aleinu*," and he added with a sigh: "You know, she died so young, just a few years ago."

"I am sorry," replied the *shamash*, "you can't say the *Kaddish*. Reb Yisroel Salanter will say *Kaddish*. Today is his father's *yahrzeit*." Mr. Isaacsohn began pleading: "But I must say *Kaddish* for my child," and he almost wept.

Reb Yisroel, who overheard the conversation, walked up to Mr. Isaacsohn and said: "Mr. Isaacsohn, *you* will say the *Kaddish* for your daughter." Noticing everyone's amazement at giving up the saying of *Kaddish* in memory of his father, Reb Yisroel turned to the congregation and said: "The mitzvah of *chessed*, doing a kindness, is far greater than the mitzvah of saying *Kaddish*."

- *Chapter Four* -

SOME OF REB YISROEL'S FAVORITE SAYINGS

- No illness is as dangerous as despair.
- Man should be first concerned with his *spiritual* needs and with his neighbor's *material* needs. Only then should he be concerned with the spiritual needs of his neighbor and his own material needs.
- The distance between the mouth and the heart is very great. Many people say great things but they do not carry them out, for their words do not flow from their hearts. However, we must not stop speaking about the great things in life, for some day our words will make an impression on our hearts and our behavior.
- The proof whether the study of *mussar* has made an impression on you is whether you are interested in studying more *mussar*.
- A businessman asked: "I can only spare one hour a day for study. Should I study Torah or *mussar* during that hour?" Reb Yisroel replied: "Study *mussar*, and you will find that you have more time for Torah study."

- Writing is easy; erasing is very difficult.
- A sick person seeks with all his power to ease his suffering. Why not do the same if his character is ailing?
- Both the *chassid* and the *misnaged* (non-*chassid*) deserve punishment. The *chassid* — for thinking that he does not need to study too much Torah because he has a Rebbe; the *misnaged* — for thinking that he needs no Rebbe because he studies Torah.
- Man is free in his imagination but must be bound by his reason.
- Many a religious man, while saying the *Shema*, thinks that Hashem is the Master of the entire universe. Yet he forgets that Hashem is also *his* master.
- Many a man, though he may live long and know much about the world around him, does not know himself.
- Every teaching of our Sages illuminates our lives like the sun at midday.
- Some people concentrate on the unimportant things in life and neglect the important ones.
- Even if we were to be punished for doing a mitzvah and rewarded for committing an *aveirah*, we would still have to do *mitzvos*.
- Man's real wealth consists of his good *middos*.
- Some people die of hunger — starving for food, but more people die heartbroken — starving for honor and glory.
- If people who do me honor would know how much I dislike to receive any form of honor, they would stop doing so.
- Though one should not seek to receive honors for himself, he must extend respect and honor to others.
- Observing a conceited person makes me feel ill.

- A man of faith should not worry about anything. The only thing he is allowed to worry about is worry itself.
- A certain orphan in Salant received no Jewish education because no one paid his tuition. Protested Reb Yisroel: "The community must sell a *Sefer Torah* and use the money to pay the orphan's tuition."
- A lonely yeshiva *bachur* lay ill in Kovno receiving no medical care. The community leaders told Reb Yisroel that they had no money for his treatment. Reb Yisroel reprimanded them: "Then sell the *paroches* and take care of the sick *bachur*."
- A yeshiva student applied to Reb Yisroel for *semichah* and prepared himself well for the expected examination. "How many volumes of the *Shulchan Aruch* have you studied?" asked Reb Yisroel. "All four volumes," answered the young candidate proudly. "Have you learned the fifth volume too?" inquired Reb Yisroel. The candidate became confused and couldn't answer, for there is no fifth volume. "Why don't you understand? The fifth volume (i.e., *mussar*) teaches you how to get along with people," said Reb Yisroel.
- Before I studied *mussar*, I used to find fault with others, not myself. Now that I have learned *mussar*, I only see my own shortcomings.
- A true community leader does not get tired of serving the people; he doesn't get angry at them; he doesn't seek to achieve greatness for himself. He only seeks to help others.

Some of Reb Yisroel's Favorite Sayings

- Chapter Five -

FOOD FOR THOUGHT

THE GREATEST GIFT

The greatest gift that Hashem gave us is the ability to learn. Learning comes from seeing, hearing, feeling, thinking, speaking, reading, writing, and much more. Among the more difficult parts of learning is the ability to analyze and understand books, experiences, and people. By analyzing, we mean not being satisfied with a simple understanding, but rather trying very hard to get the deeper and hidden meanings of whatever is being studied.

The most difficult form of learning is probably the understanding of people, especially ourselves. To understand yourself, or someone else, means to really know why a person behaves in a certain way. For example, why is one person friendly and the other not? Or why is the same person friendly and relaxed one day and angry the next day?

This book is about one of the great rabbis of the nineteenth century, Reb Yisroel Salanter. Besides for being a *tzaddik* and a *gaon*, he was the most famous master of *mussar*. Rabbi Salanter worked very hard at understanding his own behavior and continuously improving it. He also taught many people how to attain a better understanding of themselves and how to become better people. It is our hope that after having read this book, you will try to follow the example of this saintly rabbi.

WAVES AND MEN

There is something very important we can learn from the sea. We are not talking about storms and hurricanes, islands, ships, or creatures that live in the oceans. Instead, we are talking about what moral lessons we can learn from the sea.

Have you ever stood at the seashore, especially on a windy day, watching the waves? Have you noticed how restless and powerful those waves are? Most of you probably have.

Each time the waves rush toward the shore it *seems* as if they will spill over, flood the beach, and expand further and further. But usually this does not happen. The fury and energy of each wave simply vanishes when it hits the shoreline. As one set of waves breaks up, another one comes rushing toward the dry land only to fall back as the previous one did. It appears that the waves, following each other in rapid succession, never "learn" from the failures of those who came before them. It looks as if each wave "thinks" that it "knows" better how to flood the earth. But we know that the mighty ocean and its powerful waves cannot cross the boundary set by Hashem, as Dovid Hamelech wrote in *Tehillim* about the waves: "You set a boundary they cannot pass, they cannot return to cover the earth."[8] But the waves keep trying! They have not "learned" their lesson.

---

8   *Tehilim* 104:9.

Human beings may be compared to the waves of the ocean. Waves do not "remember" that others before them have tried and failed to accomplish the very thing they are now trying to do. People, too, forget to learn from the mistakes of those who lived before them.

Each generation tries to take over the world. Young people especially want to change the world and improve it. Some wish to improve the world through kindness and cooperation. Others attempt to change society by the use of force: violence, riots, revolutions, and war. It is this last group of people who refuse to learn from the mistakes of others who also tried to change the world through violence, and failed. They act unintelligently, like the waves of the sea.

Of course, we do not blame the waves for not learning from each other. But we Jews, who have a Torah, know how to learn and remember the lessons of the past.

It is the responsibility of each generation to improve the world they live in but, of course, only within the guidelines of the Torah. Just as Hashem has set limits to the mighty waters of the oceans, so did He rule that man too cannot go beyond certain limits.

In this book you have read that Reb Yisroel Salanter succeeded in making people recognize this wave-like pattern of human behavior. He taught his generation that no one can really "take over," "change," or "improve" the world without first learning how to avoid the mistakes made by others and by oneself.

One of his great teachings was that before you try to improve others, you must improve yourself. To become a successful leader, parent, or teacher, a person must first become his own master.

What does it mean to be one's own master? What does it mean to "improve" oneself? Some answers to these difficult questions may be found in this book, if you read it carefully.

Before you begin to improve yourself, you must ask yourself some questions that every religious Jew ought to think about throughout his life. Some of these questions are listed on the next page. See how you answer them.

QUESTIONS THAT CAN HELP YOU UNDERSTAND YOURSELF

This is not a test. You are not asked to answer these questions in a hurry. Try to answer these questions as honestly as you can.

1. Do you feel ashamed and sorry after having done any of the following:

   - Disobeying your parents?
   - Talking back to a teacher?
   - Refusing to share with others?
   - Looking the other way when someone needed something?
   - Arguing or fighting with your classmates, friends, or siblings?
   - Speaking *lashon hara*?
   - Being jealous of someone?
   - Cheating on a test?
   - Bragging about yourself?
   - Lying?

2. Have you felt proud and happy after having done any of the following?

   - Obeying your parents' requests right away?
   - Speaking respectfully to a teacher?
   - Sharing your things with your friends and siblings?
   - Giving *tzedakah*?
   - Not showing anger when someone upset you?

- Not speaking *lashon hara*?
- Sharing in your friend's joy?
- Helping someone in need?
- Cleaning up a mess that you didn't create?
- Telling the truth even though it is uncomfortable to do so?

3. Have you felt good after doing a mitzvah?
4. Is it important to you to have a good reputation?
5. What kind of person are you? How do you know and how do you find out?

Once you have finished reading this book, you may be able to apply some of the lessons learned to your own life. After some time has passed, try to answer the questions in this chapter again and see if anything has changed.

- *Chapter Six* -

SOME SUGGESTIONS FOR BECOMING A BETTER PERSON

THE ANSWERS YOU HAVE GIVEN TO the questions in the last chapter give you an idea of your strengths and weaknesses. This chapter, based on what we have learned from Reb Yisroel Salanter, gives you some suggestions for eliminating some of your weaknesses and adding to your strengths.

1. It is appropriate to feel guilty after having done something wrong.

One *must* be sorry if he wronged his fellow man or disobeyed Hashem. One must listen to his *yetzer hatov* in such matters, not to his desire for pleasure or revenge.

Just because a person has made mistakes in the past doesn't mean that he needs to repeat them. One must not despair from becoming a better person. As long as a person is alive ("as long as the candle burns"), he has a chance to improve himself and return to Hashem by doing *teshuvah*. Hashem loves us even when we make mistakes, and He awaits our return.

2. It is okay to be proud and happy after having done something good for someone as long as you do not become conceited.

Yes, you ought to be happy when doing a kindness to someone. In fact, this is the best way to achieve happiness. If you have not felt happy after doing a favor for someone, you have not learned yet to give of yourself. Try giving more to others — you'll likely see that it feels great!

3. Doing *mitzvos* properly always makes you feel good.

When a mitzvah has *meaning* to you, it makes you happy. You will then *want* to do it again and again.

What do we have in mind by the word "meaning?" After all, some *mitzvos*, such as *tzitzis*, *kashrus*, and *shaatnez*, are beyond man's understanding.

The answer is that *mitzvos* can have meaning if we understand that doing them brings us closer to Hashem. *The greatest pleasure man can ever attain is closeness to Hashem.*

The goal of getting closer to Hashem through Torah and *mitzvos* gives meaning to life and makes us better people. We must strive to change and improve ourselves first before we try to change and improve others. If everyone would do this, the world would become a better place to live in. Instead of fighting each other, people would then serve Hashem together.

4. A good reputation is not given free; it is earned the hard way. You must never live just for yourself. If you give help and love to others, you will be admired for it. Your name will be as good as you make it. If you keep promises, work for the welfare of others, and make the right choices, you will get a good reputation.

Some Suggestions for Becoming a Better Person

5. The best way to know yourself is to study *mussar* the way Reb Yisroel Salanter did and as his followers have been doing ever since.

To study *mussar* means more than reading such famous *mussar* books as *Shaarei Teshuvah* or *Mesillas Yesharim*, as important as they are. A person needs to be honest with himself and to watch his words and deeds. You might like to do "spiritual bookkeeping," as described in chapter 2.

In order to know yourself, you will also need to connect with your teachers and friends.

Find yourself a friend or several friends who can help make you a better person. Share your worries, your hopes, your disappointments, and your achievements with your friends. If they are true friends, they will listen and help you improve. Of course, you should do the same for them so that you will be helping each other. Sometimes you are upset or angry but you don't know why. Your friend may know *why* and tell you the reason. Chances are you will calm down and feel much better. Or, at times, you know why you are upset but you can't help yourself. A few good words from a friend are very helpful on such occasions.

All babies begin life being selfish. They are only interested in themselves and their needs and have not yet learned to care for the welfare of others. Unfortunately, some people never lose this selfish attitude.

Mussar teaches us how to focus on the needs of others rather than always thinking about our own needs and wants. Although we must place the needs of others over our own, we should not lose sight of our own worth.

When someone insults us, we should not let it affect us, and we certainly should not respond with our own insulting words. We express this idea daily in the *Shemoneh Esrei*: "Hashem, guard my tongue from evil and my lips from speaking falsehood, and to those who curse me let my soul be silent, and let my soul be unto all as dust."

What does it mean for a soul, a person, to feel like dust? It simply means that the person, being insulted or cursed by others, should not *feel* hurt just like dust cannot feel hurt. And also, just like dust never talks back, we ask Hashem to help us not return insults to those who insult us.

Notice that we ask that our soul be *like* dust but not actually *be* dust. This means that we have to *try* to act as much as possible without selfishness, but no one expects a human being to neglect himself entirely. After all, a human being has feelings, emotions, and dignity.

A person must balance his concern for himself with his involvement with others. He is neither an angel nor a selfish creature; he is a good human being. Such a man is his own master and is free to follow his *yetzer hatov*.

This is the purpose and meaning of *mussar*, as taught by Reb Yisroel Salanter.

WEEKLY CHART FOR SPIRITUAL BOOKKEEPING

Use a plus sign to represent an achievement and a minus sign to represent a failure.

VIRTUES	SUN.	MON.	TUE.	WED.	THUR.	FRI.	שבת
אֱמֶת TRUTH							
זְרִיזוּת DILIGENCE							
חֲרִיצוּת DECISIVENESS							
כָּבוֹד RESPECT							
מְנוּחַת הַנֶּפֶשׁ PEACE OF MIND							
נַחַת GENTLENESS							
נִקָּיוֹן CLEANLINESS							
סַבְלָנוּת PATIENCE							
סֵדֶר ORDERLINESS							
עֲנָוָה HUMILITY							
צֶדֶק RIGHTEOUSNESS							
קִמּוּץ THRIFT							
שְׁתִיקָה SILENCE							